Vladimir Guerrero Jr.: The Inspiring Story of One of Baseball's Star First Basemen

An Unauthorized Biography

By: Clayton Geoffreys

Copyright © 2024 by Calvintir Books, LLC

All rights reserved. Neither this book nor any portion thereof may be reproduced or used in any manner whatsoever without the express written permission. Published in the United States of America.

Disclaimer: The following book is for entertainment and informational purposes only. The information presented is without contract or any type of guarantee assurance. While every caution has been taken to provide accurate and current information, it is solely the reader's responsibility to check all information contained in this article before relying upon it. Neither the author nor publisher can be held accountable for any errors or omissions. Under no circumstances will any legal responsibility or blame be held against the author or publisher for any reparation, damages, or monetary loss due to the information presented, either directly or indirectly. This book is not intended as legal or medical advice. If any such specialized advice is needed, seek a qualified individual for help.

Trademarks are used without permission. Use of the trademark is not authorized by, associated with, or sponsored by the trademark owners. All trademarks and brands used within this book are used with no intent to infringe on the trademark owners and only used for clarifying purposes.

This book is not sponsored by or affiliated with the Major League Baseball, its teams, the players, or anyone involved with them.

Visit my website at www.claytongeoffreys.com
Cover photo by All-Pro Reels is licensed under CC BY-SA 2.0 / modified from original

Table of Contents

Foreword 1

Introduction 3

Chapter 1: Childhood and Early Years.....................12

Chapter 2: Teenage Years: Recruiting Guerrero Jr. ...23

Chapter 3: Minor League Career..............................35

Chapter 4: Major League Career 49

    Rookie Season 49

    COVID Season (2020) 63

    Vladimir Jr. Breaks Out (2021)..............................69

    Continued Success (2022-23).................................78

Chapter 5: Personal Life...88

    Nothing Beats Family..94

Chapter 6: Legacy 100

Conclusion..108

Final Word/About the Author 111

References 118

Foreword

Vladimir Guerrero Jr. made his MLB debut in 2019, and quickly established himself as one of the league's premier young talents. His notable achievements include being selected to the All-Star Game in 2021, where he made history by becoming the youngest player to win the All-Star Game MVP award. Following in the footsteps of his legendary father, a Hall of Famer, Vlad Sr., Guerrero Jr. has carved his own path to stardom. At a young age, Guerrero Jr. already a three-time All-Star and has won both Gold Glove and Silver Slugger awards.

He continues to excite fans with his dynamic play, making him one of the most exciting young stars in MLB. Thank you for purchasing *Vladimir Guerrero Jr.: The Inspiring Story of One of Baseball's Star First Basemen*. In this unauthorized biography, we will learn Vladimir Guerrero Jr.'s incredible life story and impact on the game of baseball. Hope you enjoy and if you do, please do not forget to leave a review!

Also, check out my website to join my exclusive list where I let you know about my latest books. To thank you for your purchase, I'll gift you free copies of some of my other books at **claytongeoffreys.com/goodies**.

Or, if you don't like typing, scan the QR code here to go there directly.

Cheers,

Clayton Geoffreys

Visit me at www.claytongeoffreys.com

Introduction

In the Dominican Republic, *Plákata* is slang for someone who makes strong contact with a ball resulting in an extraordinarily long home run. Fittingly, it is also the nickname for one of its most incredible athletes, a man who can hit home runs longer than almost anyone in that country—Vladimir Guerrero Jr.

"Plákata" has now been a Major League Baseball player with the Toronto Blue Jays for five years, and he is most renowned for his powerful swing that has resulted in mammoth home runs across ballparks everywhere. In his last three seasons, Guerrero Jr. has blasted a total of 106 homers, including an American League-best 48 homers in 2021.

Many say that Guerrero Jr.'s swing resembles that of Gary Sheffield; it's anything but short. Unlike Pete Alonso, who looks like he just stabs at the ball and it flies out the park, Guerrero Jr. winds up and seemingly swings for the fences every time he is at the plate, and many times, the ball does, in fact, fly out of the ballpark.

Guerrero Jr. has gained fame for a few other reasons as well. First, he is the son of a Hall-of-Fame baseball player. Vladimir Guerrero Sr. spent most of his career with the Montreal Expos and Los Angeles Angels, piling up 449 home runs. He was voted MVP in 2004, a year in which he accumulated 126 RBIs, 124 runs scored, 39 doubles, and 39 home runs. Between 1998 and 2006, Guerrero Sr. hit at least 32 home runs in all but one season. He also won seven Silver Slugger Awards and was voted to nine All-Star Games.[i]

Of course, that puts a lot of pressure on the younger Vladimir, who is trying to build his own legacy under his father's shadow. Like his father, he is beginning his career in Canada, and is exhibiting extreme power and racking up All-Star appearances.

One of the more famous pictures is one of Guerrero Sr. in an Expos uniform with his three-year-old son, both saluting the crowd, and the difference in their physiques is noticeable. Guerrero Sr. had a slim build, while Guerrero Jr. was always thicker and stockier, even as a child. That same broad build is represented today and it has led to colossal home runs.

Another reason for Guerrero Jr.'s fame is his Home Run Derby performances. In 2019, the rookie Guerrero Jr. broke the record for most home runs in one round— 29. However, that record did not even last an hour. In the next round, he shattered his own record, hitting 40. Obviously exhausted in the final round against Pete Alonso, he could only muster up 22 home runs, losing by just one. Still, the 91 home runs in one Home Run Derby set the all-time record for most in any competition.[ii]

There was no 2020 All-Star Game because of the shortened COVID-19 season, and Guerrero Jr. took the Home Run Derby off in 2021 and 2022, despite being selected for the All-Star Game. However, in 2023, he was asked to enter once again. He did, and this time, he made sure not to tire himself out. While his single-round record was broken by Julio Rodriguez, Guerrero Jr. knocked Rodriguez out in the following round and then hit 25 home runs to beat the Tampa Bay Rays' Randy Arozarena in the final.

In 2007, Vlad Guerrero Sr. had won the Home Run Derby; in 2023, his son winning it marked the first time a father and son both won the Home Run Derby. In 2024, Guerrero Jr. will seek to become the fourth player in history to repeat as Derby winner, joining Ken Griffey Jr., Yoenis Cespedes, and Pete Alonso.[ii]

But while the son is immensely proud of his heritage, he is also trying to separate from his famous father and be recognized as his own person. Junior's swing is a lot different, and many say that he has the potential to be even better. Guerrero Jr.'s wrists are faster than his father's thanks to his recent decrease in weight and he has exhibited more patience at the plate as well. He chooses his pitches more wisely, and it has led to an incredible start to his career.[iii] By all accounts, Guerrero Jr. has a great chance of out-powering his father. In 2021, he hit his 45th home run on September 12th, besting his father's single-season high.

Besides accumulating three All-Star Games already, Guerrero Jr. also has a Silver Slugger and Gold Glove to his name as a first baseman. In 2021, he led the league in seven offensive categories: runs scored (123), home runs (48), on-base percentage (.401), slugging percentage (.601), OPS (1.002), OPS+ (167), and total bases (353). He won the All-Star Game MVP and finished second for Season MVP, behind only the Angels superstar Shohei Ohtani.[iii]

Guerrero Jr. also hit .311 in 2021 and drove in 111 runs. While he has not been able to replicate that same success in the last two seasons, he has still performed at an All-Star level, hitting 32 home runs in 2022 and 26 in 2023. In five years in the league, Guerrero Jr. is hitting .279 with 130 home runs and 404 RBIs. He is slugging an impressive .490 and has already scored 377 runs. Plus, keep in mind that the 2020 season was shortened to 60 games.[ii]

Of course, having his father as a Hall-of-Famer has put the spotlight and pressure more on Vladimir Jr. to live up to the family name. It is not the first time, though. Ken Griffey Jr. had to fight his way out of his own famous father's shadow, and successfully did so in Seattle and Cincinnati. Indeed, Guerrero Jr. has used Griffey Jr. as a role model and prime example of how to handle that dynastic pressure. But his biggest attribute has perhaps been his affable and charismatic personality, maintaining positivity and always having a smile on his face. That sunny disposition has been a hallmark of his since he arrived in Toronto, and it is why so many of his teammates love being around him.

A lot of people have had a positive influence on Vladimir Jr., helping to mold him into the remarkable man he has become. His father has been a crucial mentor to him over the years, while his uncle, Wilton Guerrero, a former major league player himself, coached him in the Dominican Republic. There is also Carlos Pena, a former major leaguer who has spent some time working with him and helping him succeed.

"Vladimir Guerrero Jr. is pretty much standing on his own island," Pena said. "The sky's the limit with him."[iv]

Guerrero Jr.'s joyous and energetic personality is not something made-up, however; it is something innate that he has had since he was a child. Any picture of his youth shows him smiling and laughing, a characteristic that he has simply carried with him. No doubt, it helps deflect the pressure of expectations on his shoulders and keeps him performing at such a high level.

"I think it takes a special personality to do that," says Lee Pelekoudas, a former Mariners assistant general manager. "Vlad Guerrero Jr. could be the most talented guy in the world. But part of the blueprint is having a willingness to go out there and be the face of baseball—and have the personality to do it."[iv]

The response from Toronto has been nothing but love for Guerrero Jr., and some believe even more so than what his father had received during his time in Montreal. Guerrero Jr. has a special way of connecting with the fans and transferring his energy to them. Of course, hitting home runs helps, but it is far more than just that. After all, Alex Rodriguez hit home runs in Seattle, Texas, and New York but never got this kind of adoration. Fans absolutely love Guerrero Jr.'s smile; there's just something infectious about it. Many people compare Guerrero Jr.'s easy affability to how Derek Jeter had connected with the fans in New York.

"For the public to love you, you have to wish [for] their adulation, and you have to be lovable yourself," MLB's official historian John Thorn once said. "You can't be ornery and cantankerous and have your PR flacks project a personality different from the one you have."[iv]

But when all is said and done, Vlad Guerrero Jr.'s ultimate goal is to win a championship. He never got to see his father win one, and Toronto fans have longed to taste a World Series triumph for quite some time now. Not since Joe Carter's home run beat the Philadelphia Phillies in 1993 has Toronto earned a championship trophy. The truth is that coming out of the formidable AL East is challenging in itself, but the Toronto Blue Jays are now coming off an 89-73 season, proving that they are not far off from taking that next step. Will *Plákata* finally be the one to lead them there?

Chapter 1: Childhood and Early Years

Vladimir Guerrero Ramos Jr. was born on March 16, 1999, in Montreal, Canada, to Vladimir Guerrero Sr. and Riquelma Ramos. He later moved to the Dominican Republic after his father and mother separated. Vladimir Jr. has a brother, Pablo, who is currently signed on with the Texas Rangers.

Vladimir Jr. had the advantage of growing up with money thanks to his father's success in the major leagues. But Vladimir Sr. did not grow up with the same luxuries. Instead, he was born in a very poor neighborhood in Nizao, Dominican Republic, in a tiny house made of brick and mud, and with no roof, as they only had palm trees hanging over them thanks to a deadly hurricane in 1979, which decimated their tiny house. While Vladimir Sr. still owns that house today, it is now used as part of a tour in his hometown that his brother Wilton leads. The house is more spruced up now, with some of the Guerrero relatives living in it.

"We keep the house because we don't want to forget," Wilton said, who grew up with Vladimir Sr. and also made it to America. "We want to have it in our mind. When I come by, I say, 'Thank you, Lord,' because I have a new life now."[v]

Baseball's popularity was beginning to blossom in the Dominican Republic in the 1980s, and more and more players were making their way to the United States to play professional ball. Vladimir Sr. played baseball religiously, especially since he did not want to spend much time in his run-down neighborhood. His home life was terrible, and he regularly told his friends that he would never want his son to one day grow up in the same environment that he did.

"One hundred percent of the players that come out of the Dominican Republic are from poor families," former pitcher Pedro Martinez said. "No one that is in a wealthy position would be willing to take the amount of adversities that you have to overcome and the amount of work that you have to put in to get to the big leagues. All of us had to go through struggles. That number—*zero* wealthy persons to make it to the big leagues—it is for real."[v]

The exception, of course, is those who came from families whose parents were successful professional athletes, which would one day be the case for Vladimir Jr. and Wilton. His father and uncle, as poor as can be, worked their way up the baseball chain, and Vladimir Sr. was recruited by the Montreal Expos. In 1996, Guerrero Sr. debuted for the Expos, officially going from a poor child to a professional baseball player on the grandest of stages. It was there that he met Riquelma, and they produced Vladimir Jr. in 1999.

Vladimir Sr. and Riquelma were romantic acquaintances but never married, and they split shortly after Vladimir Jr. was born. The split was tough on young Vladimir, who went back to the Dominican Republic with his mother, who moved to Santiago.

However, his father remained a strong presence in his life, as young Vlad traveled a lot and stayed with his father during the summers, where he would often join him in the dugout.

Vladimir Sr. played his last game in Montreal in 2003, and the Expos fans, knowing that he was not going to be brought back, gave him a huge send-off at his last home game. The crowd stood and applauded him as he walked onto the Expos field for the last time, and little 3-year-old Vladimir Jr. ran out onto the field in his miniature Expos uniform and joined his dad.

"I took my hat off and everyone was still clapping," Vladimir Sr. said. "When I looked back, there was my son with his hat on. I told him, 'Now, take it off and salute the crowd.'"[v]

Vladimir Jr. did, and that picture of father and son standing there in identical light blue Expos uniforms, both with their caps in their hands and saluting the crowd is one of the most iconic pictures in MLB history. The emotion that it evokes speaks for itself, and it is a cherished image that Vladimir Jr. still looks at even today, as it sits in a huge frame in his house.

As a boy, Vladimir Jr. had a much different life than his father. Thanks to his dad, he did not grow up in a rundown neighborhood or in a house with no roof. His father made sure that his family was taken care of well, and Vlad Jr. spent a lot of time with his mother and his Uncle Wilton, who had played professional baseball for nine years with the Dodgers and Nationals and helped coach him.

Vladimir Jr. also traveled a lot, as his father went from Montreal to Los Angeles, and then eventually to Arlington, to Baltimore, and then back to the Dominican Republic. Young Vlad spent a lot of time with his grandparents as well. His grandmother, Altagracia, always called Vladimir Jr. "El Negro" because he was the darker of the two Guerrero boys.

It was Altagracia that got Vladimir Jr. into cooking at such a young age. She cooked for her grandson all the time and he could not get enough of her meals. To this day, Altagracia still cooks for her grandson and the Blue Jays, while other times Vladimir Jr. himself cooks up some of her recipes for the team.[vi]

Vladimir Jr. fell in love with the sport of baseball from the very start. Being around it constantly for some can be exhausting, but it was never so for him. He simply adored the game, and his father got him involved in it at an early age, as he was soon playing in Little Leagues and working with his Uncle Wilton, who lived in Don Gregorio, a more fancy neighborhood in Nizao.

Of course, Wilton praises his brother, Vladimir Sr., for helping him with baseball and getting him involved in the game. He was clearly able to transfer that passion for baseball to Vladimir Jr., not by force or coercion but by sheer osmosis.

"I never told him (Vladimir Jr.) to play," Vladimir Sr. said. "He's always liked it. He always had the enthusiasm to play. When I signed with Anaheim, he used to spend holidays with me, and I always took him to the stadium. I have another son and he never liked playing, so I never made him. I never forced him to play. [With Junior], that was all him."[v]

Uncle Wilton and Vladimir Jr. were extremely close, given that they spent most of the year together. He was basically a second father to him; while Vladimir Sr. was playing baseball and living most of the year in the U.S., Uncle Wilton was coaching the young boy, only sending him off to Montreal or Los Angeles during the summers and on holiday vacations.

"I think everything I've learned in baseball has been from him," Vladimir Jr. says of Wilton, "I've been practicing with him since I was five. He's the one who taught me to practice well and guided me to where I am."[v]

Just beyond Nizao, there is an old ballpark filled with grass and dirt where Vladimir Jr. would do nothing but swing for the fences every day after school. That ballpark would eventually turn into a complex with a nice fence and dirt field, which Uncle Wilton would run. There were undoubtedly times Uncle Wilton's arm got tired—he pitched 500 balls to the young boy, who just kept wanting to hit!

Vlad Jr. grew up stocky and he stayed that way, a huge difference from his father's lankier physique. He loved to eat and put on muscle, and by the time he was 10 years old, he was using those hefty muscles to hit balls deeper than most 18-year-old star players. Even if he tried to slim down as he got into his teen years, he couldn't; he was simply a different body type than his father.

"We thought that maybe because of the 'high pockets' and the long legs, maybe there's a baby fat component to this," former Blue Jays general manager Alex

Anthopoulos said, who first met Vladimir Jr. when he was just a young teenager. "Maybe he'll slim out."[v]

The best thing that happened to Vladimir Jr. was visiting his dad during the summers. It got him around the clubhouse and other major league players. By the time May came around, there may have been a sense of boredom hitting baseballs, but after being around his father and other Expos and Angels players, he came back home to the Dominican Republic with an even deeper love for the game than he had before.

"He's like his father. We're just born to play baseball," Wilton Guerrero said. "Our family was born to play this game."[vii]

As Vladimir Jr. grew up, though, he wanted to be his own person. While he adored his father and wanted to be a successful baseball player just like him, he also wanted to create his own legacy. It's the same with any son of a famous MLB player; they always want to create their own story and not be linked with someone else's. Comparisons also put

produce.

Perhaps this was the reason w
more as a role model and less o
son. He wanted young Vlad to d
with any help from him. Of cours. ...ad trained his
brother Wilton so he could relay that coaching to his
son. It was an indirect way of helping mentor Vladimir
Jr.

I sat with [Senior]," Anthopoulos reflected. "I had
been around him when I started with the Expos. He
was hands-off with his son. He did not say much. Even
if you engaged him, he deferred to Wilton on a lot of
things."[v]

Meanwhile, it was his mother, Riquelma, who helped
with all things non-baseball. While Vladimir Jr. was
obsessed with the sport and stayed mostly with his
Uncle Wilton during baseball season, she was integral
to keeping his focus on school, manners, and staying

ble. She taught her son the importance of ng others with respect.

Additionally, Riquelma had learned to speak French from living in Montreal. She passed on some of her language skills to her son, who was then able to go up to Montreal when he visited his father and more easily converse with some of the people up there, including some of his father's teammates who knew the language as well.

Chapter 2: Teenage Years: Recruiting Guerrero Jr.

Rumors were spreading fast around the Dominican Republic about a young and powerful phenom who was the son of an MLB great. Uncle Wilton, with the guidance of Vladimir Sr., had turned a young Vladimir Guerrero Jr. into a machine who was pounding home runs over the fence and into the mountains of Nizao.

Because of his name, scouts were all over young Vladdy at just 12 years old as he was performing at Wilton Guerrero's Baseball Academy, funded by Vladimir Guerrero Sr. They were keeping an eye on him, watching him develop, and talking to Uncle Milton and expressing interest. Local scouts sent word of the young teenager's progress to their regional and international MLB scouts, who then relayed those messages to their front offices.

A few teams were more interested than others, notably the Texas Rangers and Toronto Blue Jays. Gil Kim was the Rangers' international scout, and he could not help but be pulled back to the Dominican Republic to watch Guerrero Jr. hit.

"There was this little guy out there in right field, and then in the infield, and then hitting bombs," Kim recalled as he watched Guerrero Jr. play.[viii]

Kim worked all of Central America, including Mexico and Puerto Rico, but the talent pool in the Dominican Republic had constantly been growing in the 2000s. Players like Albert Pujols, Starling Marte, Ervin Santana, Carlos Pena, Hanley Ramirez, and Juan Uribe were just a few of the big names in recent years to come out of the country. The list kept growing.

"You're routinely wowed and amazed by the talents and abilities of younger players," Kim said. "The Dominican is a fascinating place to watch, to see how talented baseball players develop. With Vladdy, maybe the awe factor was a little more."[viii]

The Toronto Blue Jays were also obsessed with watching the powerful young teenager compete. They watched in amazement as Guerrero Jr. smacked long home runs against guys who were some 5-to-10 years older than him and likely poised for greatness themselves.[vii]

But the man who probably kept eyes on him the most was Ismael Cruz, the head of the Blue Jays Latin American scouting. He had been monitoring Guerrero Jr. since he was 12 years old and was already dreaming of signing him when he was old enough, with the general manager's consent, of course. He was so enamored with Guerrero Jr., that, by the time the young star was 14 years old, Cruz had called his general manager, Alex Anthopoulos, and asked him to come down to watch him and some of the other young burgeoning talents in the Dominican Republic. When Anthopoulos watched Vladdy practice, he was in awe of what he was seeing.

"We didn't know the names, they were just these kids hitting, and Vlad comes up and he's just hitting balls, loose, quick, easy swing, balls jumping off his bat," Anthopoulos said.[viii]

When Anthopoulos asked Cruz who the big kid was pounding home runs out over the fence, Cruz responded, "That's Vlad Guerrero Sr.'s kid."[viii]

Guerrero Jr. played in games and tournaments throughout the country and was by far one of the best hitters and most scouted players. He practiced a lot with his uncle down at his father's field, continuing to showcase his power. By the time he was 15, curiosity in the young slugger was growing exponentially, as he was now closing in on the important age of 16, which is when the MLB dictates an international player can sign with an MLB club.

Anthopoulos told Cruz to keep an eye on him, and, as time went on, more MLB teams' scouts showed interest in Guerrero Jr. Alex Anthopoulos visited the

Dominican once again in the summer of 2014, increasingly interested in signing the young star when it was time. Then, New Year's Eve came, and it had gotten to the point where the Blue Jays had to act fast. There was going to be a big showcase going on at the Wilton Guerrero Complex on January 1, 2015, and Cruz called Anthopoulos and told him that he needed to come down for it or they would risk losing him to someone else.

"I remember just looking at my wife and saying I'm not going to be able to be here for New Year's Day," Anthopoulos said. "So, on New Year's Day, I got on a plane, went to the Dominican, Ismael picked me up, we went to see Vladdy work out at his father's field."[ix]

Anthopoulos took time to get to know Guerrero Jr. more personally. The first thing that stood out to him was his personality; he was easy to talk to, happy, jovial, and had a carefree spirit. He stood out as the kind of teammate who would pull the rest of the team together. You could not help but like him. He did not pay as much attention to his last name, either, whereas some teams did.

"There have been plenty of guys who have been related to major league players or sons with bloodlines who haven't worked out," Anthopoulos explained. "I think there's value to it. He had an appreciation of what the life was like and what was involved. But skills are skills and ability is ability. He wasn't his father. It wasn't the same body. They weren't the same guy at all.[v]

"But what we really liked was the fact that he grew up with money," Alex continued. "We liked the fact that playing baseball for him wasn't about getting off the island and feeding his family. He played baseball because he loved it. Everything he did, his love for the game, was really authentic. He was going to *will* himself, *drive* himself, because he really loved playing."[v]

It was a valid point. Guerrero Jr. did not need to play baseball to make a living for himself like some athletes. Many guys from the Dominican work hard because they have nothing. They often want to play their way into the majors so they can make money and change their way of life, not only for themselves but also for their families. But Guerrero Jr. already had that financial security from his father; he never really needed to work in his life and he would be fine. Instead, he worked hard and was motivated to play because he loved the game, not because of the paychecks involved.

It went without saying that the Blue Jays were now all-in on signing Guerrero Jr. They had to verify his age, though, and make sure that they did not sign him prematurely. (This was critical, because many Dominican Republic players tend to lie about their age just to get signed early, and it ultimately penalizes the organization.) So, they drove three hours to meet Riquelma in Santiago, Vladimir Jr.'s mother. On the car ride there, Anthopoulos noticed that Guerrero Jr. was watching something on his phone and was curious about what it was.

"He was watching highlights of his dad," Anthopoulos said. "He has never said this to me, but he idolizes his dad. He was so proud to show me some of the highlights—the defensive plays, the hits. You could tell he really wanted to emulate everything his dad did."[v]

Since Anthopoulos was French himself, he was able to connect with Riquelma, and the two spoke to each other in French at the meeting. One of the things that Guerrero Jr. noticed in the meeting was just how good the connection was between his mom and the Blue Jays general manager.

"We knew the date of birth was accurate because he was born in Quebec," Anthopoulos said. "His mother, when we were at her house, she was very proud, she brought out his Quebec birth certificate."[viii]

Riquelma was a big influence on Vladimir Jr.'s eventual destination, and it was she who gave the approval after meeting with the Blue Jays general manager. Further in their favor was the fact that the Jays were willing to let him play third base, which is what his preferred position was. But there were still more workouts to go through and meetings to be had.

Just before Spring Training in 2015, the Blue Jays coordinated with Edwin Encarnacion, their current first baseman and one of their top players with ties in the Dominican Republic, to secure a private field without anyone knowing. It would be a private workout with important people in the organization and Encarnacion in attendance to watch Guerrero Jr. hit.

The Blue Jays brought in one of their best international pitching prospects, Yadier Alvares, who had a 100-mph fastball. Despite the age difference and top talent from Alvares, he still could not put it by Guerrero Jr. Pitch after pitch, the ball was just getting crushed.

Encarnacion nodded to the Blue Jays top guys and advised them to sign the kid.

"We put him in difficult situations where anybody else will fail," Cruz said.[vii]

Obviously, Guerrero Jr. did not. Anthopoulos also held a workout with Guerrero Sr. present and had a private conversation with him, wanting to learn more about the son from the father. Anthopoulos continued to come away impressed as he watched the young boy not only hit with power and display great defense but also showcase a smile and joyful grin all throughout his time playing. He was clearly loving the game.

"I sat with [Senior]," Anthopoulos reflected. "I had been around him when I started with the Expos. He was hands-off with his son. He did not say much. Even if you engaged him, he deferred to Wilton on a lot of things."[v]

At just 16 years old, Guerrero Jr. was *Baseball America's* top-ranked international prospect;

32

meanwhile, MLB.com had him ranked No. 4. The Blue Jays were one of three teams most aggressively pursuing Guerrero Jr. on his 16th birthday. The other two that the 16-year-old was talking to included the Rangers and Chicago White Sox.

Guerrero Jr. liked the Blue Jays, but the challenge for Anthopoulos and their front office was affording the young superstar. Teams are only allocated a specific amount of money ($2.6 million) for the international signing pool. Thus, the Blue Jays had to make a shrewd trade, dealing two of their international prospects to the Dodgers, to be able to pay for Guerrero Jr. without suffering a severe tax penalty.[x]

In the end, Guerrero Jr. and the Blue Jays agreed on a $3.9-million signing bonus on July 2, 2015. The Blue Jays received $1 million in return in their trade with the Dodgers. They would still incur a penalty for going over the budget but it would not be as severe since they only went over slightly.

"It was either play all your marbles on one guy or go out and get a couple of players who are fine, but for us, Vladdy Jr. is a difference maker," Cruz said. "He has the potential to be a very, very special kid."[x]

Chapter 3: Minor League Career

Vladimir Guerrero Jr.'s professional career would begin in Dunedin, Florida, debuting at the Blue Jays' minor league complex as a 16-year-old. Eventually, he would be sent to the Appalachian Rookie League in Bluefield, West Virginia.

For most 16-year-olds, this would be an overwhelming experience, being the young kid around a bunch of 20-something-year-olds with a ton of talent. Being the son of a Hall-of-Famer added even more pressure, as people were expecting to see greatness because of his name. But Guerrero Jr. had been around this kind of atmosphere before with his father; this was nothing new to him. He showed up with the same big smile and easy confidence that he had displayed at Uncle Wilton's complex in Don Gregorio.

"Since I was a little kid, I played with a lot of people watching me," Guerrero Jr. said. "Sometimes—

sometimes—I feel pressure. But sometimes you just notice a lot of people looking at you."[xi]

As people showed up to watch some of the prospects' scrimmage games, they came away most impressed by the young boy who had immense expectations on him. At 6'1" and 200 pounds, he was a sight to behold. His batting practice sessions were most impressive, as the crack of the bat could be heard a mile away. One morning, he launched a home run over the left-field fence, over the trees, and onto a nearby softball field used by recreational teams. When asked what uniform number he wanted, he did not hesitate—No. 27, the same number his father wore.

As Guerrero Jr. turned 17, he headed to West Virginia to play in the rookie league. The only concern the team seemed to have was with his weight, as evidenced by the weight program they put him on. But he had shown incredible promise as an infielder, and of course, as a hitter. He brought a sense of excitement to the Blue Jays clubhouse that they had not felt in a long time.

"He's going to be fun to watch, I'll tell you that," Gil Kim said, who, in the offseason, was signed by the Blue Jays as their director of player development.[xii]

"He's a little more advanced than most 17-year-old international free-agent signings," Kim continued. "He has raw power, hand-eye coordination, and baseball feel. He's a confident player who's working hard on improving his athleticism and overall body strength. The mechanics are good, but really, it's his natural talent, mentality, and approach that make him advanced for his age."[xi]

Baseball America had him ranked as the No. 1 international prospect; by the time he started the Appalachian League, they had him at No. 3 overall for all prospects, international and domestic. The only question now was, how long would he spend in the minors before being brought up to the major leagues?

If all went well, he'd only have to spend two or three years in the farm system before being called up to Toronto.[xii]

Guerrero Jr.'s father was in attendance when he got his first hit, a two-run single in the bottom of the seventh that helped lift his team to a 9-4 win. Later in the game, he would also record his first professional home run, much to his father's excitement. He would hit another one just a couple of nights later.

"I felt no pressure after yesterday's game and was able to stay focused today," Guerrero Jr. said. "Staying focused was something I watched my dad do growing up, so I was ready for the challenge. I always talk to my dad before and after games, even when he's not there watching me. We talked before today and he really didn't have any specific advice. He just encouraged me, mostly."[xiii]

"I didn't want him to see me," his father said. "I didn't want to pressure him. I didn't want him to have me take away from that. But I had to go to the ballpark to check it out."[xiv]

Guerrero Jr. would ultimately play 62 games in the Appalachian Rookie League, and his time there produced mixed results. While his average was not overly impressive at .271, he was an all-around talent. He had 8 home runs and 12 doubles to go along with 46 RBIs. He also displayed excellent speed for a player of his size, stealing 15 bases. His raw power and impressive physique meant players tried to pitch around him and get him to chase, but Guerrero Jr. was very disciplined. He drew 33 walks while striking out 35 times.[ii]

"In spring training, I felt really lost," he said. "My timing wasn't too good. But once extended started, and the coaches kept working with me, my shoulder was staying a lot closer, a lot tighter. I started working toward hitting to the middle and right side of the field a lot more."[xv]

But while his average was a bit of a disappointment in 2016, it would not be an issue in 2017, when Guerrero Jr. saw a massive surge in production. He began the year in Lansing, Michigan, playing A-Ball in the Midwest League. There, he would team up with another young Blue Jays top prospect, Bo Bichette, another son of a great MLB player. The two of them would give Lansing a major power surge.

Guerrero Jr. hit .316 in Lansing with seven home runs and 45 RBIs in 71 games played. He added 21 doubles and scored 53 runs. He and Bichette were chosen to play in the MLB Futures Game in Miami. By mid-season, Guerrero Jr. had moved up to being the No. 2 ranked prospect by *Baseball America*.[xiv]

Dante Bichette, the father of Bo who worked as a special assistant of the Blue Jays at the time, had seen a lot of Guerrero Jr.'s games and was able to relay what he was seeing to the rest of the front office.

"I think I know who the best hitter in baseball is, but he's not in the big leagues," Bichette remembered telling the team. "And that's what I truly thought … 'This kid, once he gets to the big leagues, he's going to blow up.'"[vii]

Guerrero Jr.'s production propelled the Blue Jays to move him to A+ Ball in the Florida State League in Dunedin, along with Bichette. In 48 games, he shined, hitting .333 and adding six home runs. Between both teams, he compiled an impressive .485 slugging percentage and .425 on-base percentage.[ii]

Guerrero Jr. appeared in the Futures Game for the second straight season and showcased himself on national television, going 2-for-4 with two runs scored. The youngest kid on the roster was making his father proud, even though Guerrero Sr. wanted to try and tamper expectations because he knew how hard it was on his son.

After a successful 2017 season, Guerrero Jr. wanted to keep improving. He headed back down to the Dominican Republic to play in the Dominican Winter League, where his Uncle Wilton along with other Blue Jays coaches helped him improve his defense and continue to get better as a hitter. The league was mostly an instructional league with the purpose of helping players in specific areas—in this case, Guerrero Jr. with his defense.

Guerrero Jr., though, for the first time, showed signs of fatigue and struggled at the plate, hitting just .211 in 26 games. He failed to homer and produced just two doubles in 90 at-bats. Still, the main focus was improving his defense, which he did in the winter.

Just before Spring Training ended, the Blue Jays called Guerrero Jr. up to the main roster for an exhibition double-header in Montreal against the St. Louis Cardinals. While he did not get a hit in the first game, he hit a walk-off homer to win the game for the Blue

Jays 1-0. The crowd of over 25,000 went crazy and got déjà vu, as they saw a No. 27 with the last name Guerrero on the back of the jersey circle the bases.[ii]

The Blue Jays continued to elevate Guerrero Jr. after a solid 2017 season, moving him to AA-Ball in New Hampshire to play for the Blue Jays' affiliate in the Eastern League. For the first month, he absolutely tore the cover off the ball. Guerrero Jr. was turning 19 and was finally on the cusp of playing his way into the major leagues.

In his first 79 at-bats in the Eastern League, Guerrero Jr. was hitting .380 with an impressive .582 slugging percentage. His strikeout numbers were way down while he continued to exhibit patience and draw walks. Scouts who were watching him continued to chime in that "he was ready."[xvi]

Of course, the Blue Jays had decisions to make. Josh Donaldson was their third baseman at the top level, and while Guerrero Jr. enjoyed playing third base, he was open to switching to first base or designated hitter if it meant moving up to the major league roster earlier. He got some work in at first base in New Hampshire, although he still primarily stayed as a third baseman.

Guerrero Jr. did not let up in May or June, and through 62 games in the Eastern League, he was hitting a league-best .402 with 14 home runs and 60 RBIs. Fans in New Hampshire were showing up just to watch him play and hit rockets off of pitchers. Unfortunately, fans did not get to see him for long, because by July, Guerrero had moved his way up to AAA with the Buffalo Bison in the International League.[ii]

"He's the best I've ever seen, hands down," New Hampshire manager John Schneider said about Guerrero Jr.[xvii]

"He's done a really good job of making his own way and being his own dude," Schneider continued, discussing him living in his father's shadow and dealing with the media expectations and pressure.

"Obviously it's not easy to deal with, but he's doing great with it."[xviii]

There was discussion of moving Guerrero Jr. up to the top level in Toronto at that time, but the Blue Jays front office held off on that move, not wanting to start his career off in the middle of the season. When they brought him up, they wanted it to be for good.

Meanwhile, Guerrero Jr. was making headlines in Buffalo. He had transformed into a disciplined hitter, making it hard for pitchers to throw against him because he simply would not chase. It was something he had learned when he was a boy. Even when Blue Jays scouts had visited him, they would notice how he was so engrossed in the game, watching the man on the mound hard while he was in the dugout. He was the same way in the minor leagues.

"He studied pitchers," Ismael Cruz said. "At 15, he had a plan going into the box. He would tell us, 'This guy uses this pitch to go for a strikeout. I want to make him believe he's got me on the first breaking ball, then get him on the second one.' Stuff you don't hear from a 15-year-old kid. [xviii]

Home runs kept firing off Guerrero Jr.'s bat in Buffalo. On August 10th, he homered for the third straight game, helping his team rally to win 5-4. The next night, he homered again, making it four straight games with a homer. It lifted his batting average at the time to an incredible .433. [ii]

"Everybody does a little something great, he does all of it," Bison hitting coach Corey Hart said. "He's ready to hit every time, he has great strike zone discipline ... He has a better strike zone than the umpire most of the time. "He's very, very strong and he's got a great swing. But hands down, the most important one is he's a fierce competitor."[xix]

Guerrero Jr., who was now the No. 1-ranked prospect in the minor leagues according to pretty much every publication, hit .336 in 30 games with Buffalo in AAA.

Peter Gray	Peter Gray	Peter Gray	Peter Gray
Peter Gray	Peter Gray	Peter Gray	Peter Gray
Peter Gray	Peter Gray	Peter Gray	Peter Gray
Peter Gray	Peter Gray	Peter Gray	Peter Gray
Peter Gray	Peter Gray	Peter Gray	Peter Gray
Peter Gray	Peter Gray	Peter Gray	Peter Gray

Scotch Film

He hit seven doubles and six home runs in 110 at-bats. Overall, in 2018, between AA and AAA, Guerrero Jr. hit .381 and finished with an astounding .636 slugging percentage. He compiled 29 doubles and 20 home runs in 95 total games. He walked 37 times while striking out just 38.[ii]

Guerrero Jr.'s incredible 2018 season led him to be named *Baseball America's* Minor League Player of the Year. He became just the second Blue Jays player to ever win the honor, and the first since Derek Bell in 1991. He also followed an impressive list of players who had won the award in recent years, including Ronald Acuna Jr. in 2017, Alex Bregman in 2016, Blake Snell in 2015, Kris Bryant in 2014, and Xander Bogaerts in 2013.[xx]

The question now seemed to be, where would Guerrero Jr. play with the Blue Jays? It was hard to find a weakness, although some in the media tried to say it was his defense. His manager in Buffalo disagreed, though.

"I see his footwork and how he moves to make the plays and his arm strength, and there is no doubt he can play third base," the Buffalo manager said. "He is moving better than guys smaller than him. The first step is huge for the third baseman, and we keep track of his improvement with video, and you can see his progress."[xx]

The belief was that Guerrero Jr. would almost certainly begin the season with the Toronto Blue Jays and be a major leaguer. He was most definitely ready.

Chapter 4: Major League Career

Rookie Season

Vladimir Guerrero Jr. spent Spring Training in Dunedin, Florida, with the main roster, working with the coaches and getting himself ready to be the starting third baseman. The team had traded away Josh Donaldson, paving the way for a potential Opening Day start for the 19-year-old. However, general manager Ross Atkins poured a little water on the fire by saying he wasn't sure Guerrero Jr. would be ready to start in the majors. Many, though, saw that as him deliberately tampering with expectations, as league rules state that a team can get an extra year of control over a player if they wait at least 15 days before calling up a prospect.

Guerrero Jr. started Spring Training doing well, but on March 10th, three weeks before the season started, he suffered an oblique strain. Out of caution, the team sidelined him for the rest of Spring Training. The three-week injury gave the Blue Jays a valid reason to keep him in the minors for an extra 15 days.

"In his last at-bat, he felt a sharp pain in his side, which for the first time for any young player is a frightening feeling, and fortunately, it is just a Grade 1 and it's something we'll be able to manage," Atkins said.[xxi]

When the Blue Jays began the season, Guerrero Jr. stayed in Dunedin, working with the Florida State League in a rehab operation. After four games, he went 4-for-15 with a double and two walks. Thus, the team promoted him to AAA in Buffalo again.

Guerrero played nine games in the International League, hitting .367 with a double and three colossal homers that brought the crowd to their feet. Guerrero Jr. knew that, after a couple of weeks, a call could come at any moment bringing him up to the major leagues.

That call came on April 24, 2019.

"It's a big moment for the Toronto Blue Jays," manager Charlie Montoyo said. "He's the No. 1 prospect in baseball and he's coming on Friday so it's a big moment for us. Hopefully, he becomes what everybody thinks he's going to become and that's going to be good for all of us—for the city of Toronto, the Blue Jays, the organization."[xxii]

Montoyo did not want to break the news to him personally, however. Instead, he let the guys he was closest to, Bison manager Bobby Meachem and personnel director Gil Kim, tell him the good news. When his father heard the good news, he sent out a post on social media with the famous picture of him and his three-year-old son saluting the crowd in their Expos uniforms.

"My son! The country that saw you as a child will now see you turn into a big one. Working hard, everything can be done. I'm proud of you. Love you."[xxii]

Guerrero headed to Toronto, and on April 26th, put on the Blue Jays home jersey for the first time. When he went in front of the media before the game, many said he looked like a guy who wasn't about to play his first major league game. He looked like a veteran already used to the spotlight.

"Since I was a kid, I was running around with my dad in the clubhouse in Montreal," Guerrero Jr. said through a translator. "I just wanted to bring that back today. I'm very happy, very proud of making my debut in Canada."[xxiii]

The first three at-bats did not go the way Guerrero Jr. wanted them to, but his final at-bat of the day was what he would remember most when he looked back at his first game. Facing Oakland and with the game tied at 2-2, Guerrero Jr. led off the ninth inning. On a 2-2 fastball from Yusmeiro Petit, Guerrero Jr. connected with the pitch and lined it up the right-field line for a double. Two hitters later, Brandon Drury hit a home run to win the game for the Blue Jays.

"Just the way I dreamed it," Guerrero said with a big smile.[xxiv]

"He's a great player," Drury said. "You can see by his at-bats the game kind of comes easy to him. We're all super excited to have Vladdy in this lineup."[xxiv]

Guerrero Jr. was given a thunderous ovation after the game by the crowd, who had high expectations for him. He did not disappoint. The next night, he got another hit and drew a walk in a 7-1 Blue Jays win. Guerrero Jr. started his career with a three-game hitting streak, helping the Blue Jays win again 5-4 in 11 innings against the A's.[ii]

"I'm just very happy," Guerrero said through a translator. "I'm trying to help the team with everything I can."[xxv]

You could see the happiness in him, too. The fans loved his smile and carefree personality. He looked like he was having fun out there and the players clearly loved having him in the dugout.

Guerrero Jr. hit a bit of a slump after the hot start, however, and went into the Blue Jays' May 14th road game in San Francisco hitting just .191. He had yet to homer, and at 16-24, the team was also going through a rough skid in a difficult division. Frustrated with his play, Guerrero Jr. received some advice from his father to get him through the rough stretch. He used the advice well.

On May 14th, Guerrero Jr. not only hit his first home run as a major leaguer, he hit two in the same game. He became the youngest player ever in Blue Jays history to hit a home run, and the third youngest MLB player ever to hit his first two home runs in the same game. He added another hit, making it a three-for-four night with four RBIs. His father's advice was a wonder.[xxvi]

"He just said like he always told me, `Don't look for home runs. They're going to come," Guerrero said through a translator. "I'm going to give both balls and the bat to my dad. I'm going to keep using everything that I used today except the bat that I really want to give to my dad."[xxvi]

"He was talking about it during batting practice and he did it," Toronto manager Charlie Montoyo said. "We knew that was coming. He's that good. He could carry a team if he gets hot. He can do stuff like that."[xxvi]

The first home run was not a short one, either. The ball traveled 438 feet and was measured at 111.3 mph off his bat.

The home runs began to take off from there. A couple of nights later, Guerrero Jr. blasted another shot, followed by another two nights after that. In all, he hit six home runs in May and was a big bright spot in

Toronto despite their awful record. From May 14th to May 31st, Guerrero Jr. had six multi-hit games, including four three-hit games. He boosted his average in that time from .191 to .248.[ii]

Guerrero Jr. faced some struggles defensively, though, and the Blue Jays used him more in the designated hitter role to give him a break. On June 5th against the Yankees, Guerrero Jr., hitting in the DH role, continued to find his rhythm at the plate. Trailing in the eighth inning, Guerrero Jr. blasted a home run off of Yankees pitcher Zack Britton to put the Blue Jays ahead for good. It ended up being the winning home in an 11-7 victory.[ii]

On June 12th and June 13th, Guerrero Jr. combined to go six-for-nine against the Orioles with two doubles and two RBIs. While his home run numbers slowed down during the month, he avoided going into a major slump during the month and kept the excitement going in Toronto.

While Vlad had his struggles in the first two months, he was still creating a lot of buzz around the league. On June 30th, he received an invitation from the MLB to compete in the July 8th Home Run Derby in Cleveland, making him the youngest player ever to compete in the event.

Guerrero Jr. went into the All-Star break hitting .249 with 8 home runs and 35 RBIs. But he would generate a lot of noise at the Home Run Derby. The historic night in Cleveland began in the opening round when Guerrero Jr. hit 29 home runs against the A's Matt Chapman, the most any competitor has hit in any round in Derby history. He hit five home runs over 450 feet, two homers over 460 feet, and a 476-foot shot; he also went on a string of four dingers in a row.[xxvii]

However, it was the second-round battle that garnered the most buzz against Joc Pederson. Guerrero Jr.'s 29 homers for one round was tied by Pederson who hit 29; however, Guerrero Jr. matched that, hitting 29 of his own, including a 488-foot colossal home run. His average home run distance in the round was a record 422.8 feet.

The two sluggers went into a tiebreaker round where they both hit eight home runs, sending it into another tiebreaker. Eventually, Guerrero Jr. beat Pederson 40-39 in an epic battle. All throughout the round, Cleveland fans were chanting, "Let's go Vladdy!"[xxvii]

"That wasn't exciting because you just want to win," Guerrero Jr. said, with a smile. "He kept tying me and I was just scared that he was going to beat me. I told him, 'I thought you were going to beat me,' and he said, 'You beat me, but I was already exhausted.'"[xxvii]

Guerrero's tiebreaker with Pederson took a toll on him, however. Obviously exhausted, he still hit an impressive 22 home runs in the final, but seemingly ran out of gas. The Mets' Pete Alonso hit 23 home runs to win the Home Run Derby.

"I got tired, but that's not why I lost," Guerrero Jr. said. "There are no excuses. [Alonso] hit more home runs than me and he won."[xxvii]

Despite finishing as runner-up, Guerrero Jr. broke the record for most home runs during any Home Run Derby with 91. And perhaps even more gratifying was the fact that Guerrero Jr. had clearly won over the crowd, who were chanting his name all throughout the final and after.

"First of all, you just have to thank God and the fans for all the support," Guerrero Jr. said after breaking the record. "We gave everyone a good show, and that's what we wanted ... I feel proud of hitting 91 home runs because I broke the record."[xxvii]

It wouldn't be Guerrero Jr.'s last Home Run Derby moment during his career. After the All-Star break, Guerrero Jr. went on a hot run. On July 20th, he hit his first grand slam, a 441-foot blast that helped erase a 5-1 deficit to propel the Blue Jays to a 7-5 victory.

"That's the Vladdy that we know," Blue Jays manager Charlie Montoyo said. "That's what he can do, and that's what we're waiting for, everybody was waiting for. He's looking good at the plate now."[xxviii]

Guerrero Jr. also hit a home run and four RBIs to help rally the Blue Jays from a 9-2 deficit to win 10-9 over the Tampa Bay Rays on July 27th. Despite his average hovering around .260, Guerrero ended July with his slugging percentage at .430 for the season. His 20 RBIs were a team-high during the month of July.[ii]

Between July 27th and August 4th, Guerrero Jr. got 18 hits and 18 RBIs in eight games, and the accolades for him were only growing. On July 30th, he hit his second grand slam in 10 days in a 9-2 win over the Royals.

"He's getting hot now and I knew that was going to happen," Montoya said. "He's seeing the ball better. He's having good at-bats. He wasn't doing that and still getting hits because he's just that good, but now he's having good at-bats."[xxix]

Guerrero lifted his average all the way to .279 and thrust his name into the Rookie of the Year race. He hit .341 in August with four home runs, 16 RBIs, and a .571 slugging percentage.[ii] But he then went through a challenging September wherein he simply ran out of gas. Over the final two months, the Blue Jays increasingly rested Guerrero Jr. as they saw him suffering from fatigue. He hit just .232 and failed to hit a home run during the month. The Blue Jays' struggles as a team also were not helping his chances as they continued to lose games, falling to 35 games under .500.

"We could see he was tired from time to time and that's why he played less," general manager Ross Atkins said of the situation. "Based on his reporting weight we did expect some level of that."[xxx]

Guerrero Jr. finished on a bit of a run at the end of the year, getting four two-hit games in a row after a bit of a rest, helping boost his average some. He finished his rookie campaign hitting .272 with 15 home runs and 69 RBIs. Additionally, he compiled 26 doubles, scored 52 runs, and slugged .433. The Blue Jays finished the year in last place in their division at 65-95.

Guerrero Jr., who was the favorite to win the award before the season started, finished sixth in the final Rookie of the Year voting, with Yordan Alvarez of the Astros winning the honor. While Guerrero Jr. had solid hitting numbers, it was his fielding and base-running skills that were disappointing. Guerrero Jr. had just a .936 fielding percentage and produced 17 errors, a league high for third basemen. His Fielding Runs Above Average was a disappointing -16, another reason for the team resting him more at the end of the year.[ii]

"I think he was great," Montoyo said. "The problem was the expectations were too much, it wasn't fair. He's 20 years old. To hit .270 with 15 home runs is not bad. Every time he goes to the plate people expect so much, but he's 20. Also, he'd never played in September, you can run out of gas, which he did a little bit. You can learn from all of that."[xxx]

COVID Season (2020)

The biggest concern surrounding Guerrero Jr. was his weight and fitness. For the longest time, his size represented power to many, but now in the majors, some saw the drawbacks of it as well. Guerrero Jr. could hit, no doubt, but he had to catch up to the speed of the game in other areas.

After the 2019 season ended, the Blue Jays told Guerrero Jr. to report to Spring Training in 2020 in better physical condition. Thus, he spent a lot of time trying to trim down and get himself into elevated shape.

Subsequently, Guerrero Jr. showed up to Spring Training in excellent shape, the best of his baseball career. But just as he was getting ready for the season, disaster struck—the COVID-19 pandemic. The deadly virus shut down all sports, including baseball, and people were urged to isolate themselves to slow the spread. Guerrero Jr. traveled back to the Dominican Republic and because he was not able to go out or do much, his fitness declined once again.

By the time Guerrero Jr. returned to the U.S. after it was safe to travel back, it was already July and the MLB announced that they would play a shortened 60-game season. The teams reported back for a shortened Spring Training, and the Blue Jays immediately noticed that the slimmed-down version of Guerrero Jr. from February was out of shape again in July. Some reports listed the overweight Guerrero Jr. at 282 pounds.

"We didn't really have any doubts that he'd get in shape, at least I didn't," teammate Bo Bichette said. "I've always known the determination he has to be the best. And I was pretty positive that he wasn't going to show up and not be in the best possible situation he could be to produce at a high level."[vii]

Guerrero Jr. immediately apologized, having gained some 50 pounds during the pandemic. The truth of the matter was that Guerrero Jr., like most all baseball players, did not even think there was going to be a season; it seemed lost. So, he enjoyed his grandmother's meals, thinking he wouldn't have to report to camp for another year. But then he got the surprise call that there was going to be a season.

The Blue Jays came up with a plan to try and help Guerrero Jr.'s defensive play given his physique. During the offseason, they began working with him a little bit at first base, a position that would benefit his size more. The third base position required more quickness, which Guerrero Jr. struggled with given his size. At first, it was a move they were not sure about, but after showing up overweight on July 10th, Charlie Montoya announced it would be a permanent move.

Another problem the Blue Jays were dealing with was that they were not allowed to travel to Toronto once the season started. Because of the pandemic, there were travel restrictions in place, and the Blue Jays, being the only Canadian team, were left without a home. They would end up playing the 2020 season in Buffalo at their AAA affiliate's field.

Many stadiums around the league restricted fans from attending games, meaning the Blue Jays played games in front of no fans, including in New York, where the quarantine regulations were the strictest. It would make the season very peculiar for Guerrero Jr. and the entire team.

Guerrero Jr. had a challenging Spring Training and started the shortened year in a slump. He hit just .172

in July, going 5-for-29 with just one home run and one RBI. While he picked it up some in August, he was still hovering around .240 for most of the month.[ii]

Going into the team's August 25th contest with the Red Sox, Guerrero Jr. was hitting just .245 with just four home runs and eight RBIs on the year. Still, the expanded playoffs because of the shortened season kept the Blue Jays in contention for a Wild Card spot. But then, things began improving for Guerrero Jr. He went on a 12-game hitting streak, the longest of his career, and from August 25th to August 30th, recorded eight hits and nine RBIs in five games. At 18-14, the postseason was suddenly looking promising.[ii]

On September 21st against the Yankees, Guerrero Jr. doubled twice and drove in three runs to lift the Blue Jays to an 11-5 win. After another three-RBI performance against the Yankees two days later, he closed out the series going 3-for-4 with a home run, helping lift the Blue Jays to the point that they were on the cusp of the playoffs.

Guerrero Jr. finished the shortened season hitting .262 with 9 home runs and 33 RBIs. While he struggled in many categories compared to 2019, his slugging percentage improved to .462. He also started every single game for the Blue Jays and helped them make the playoffs. Defensively, he also seemed to find more comfort at first base.

The Blue Jays would face a difficult challenge, going up against the AL East champion Tampa Bay Rays. Guerrero Jr. struggled against the dynamic Rays pitchers, going 1-for-7 in the two games. The Rays swept the Jays in the three-game series, winning both games convincingly. The Rays went on to win the American League but ultimately lost the World Series to the Los Angeles Dodgers.[ii]

The media was quick to criticize Guerrero Jr. again for showing up overweight, although COVID-19 had played a big role in that. Nevertheless, the Blue Jays wanted Guerrero Jr. to come back in 2021 in much better shape. Vlad promised that he would—and he would deliver on that promise to produce an MVP-caliber season.

Vladimir Jr. Breaks Out (2021)

Guerrero Jr. showed up to Spring Training in Dunedin more than 42 pounds lighter and in much better shape than he did after the pandemic in 2020. His hard work back in the Dominican Republic had paid off, and he showed off his power in Spring Training with some electrifying home runs. Because of all the weight he lost, he was swinging through the ball more quickly. But the biggest impact was in his arms—his wrists were so fast it was hard to get anything past him!

Unfortunately, the Blue Jays still did not have a home, as COVID travel restrictions were still in place. Thus, the Blue Jays announced that they would start the season at their Spring Training home in Dunedin and move to Buffalo in June.

The media had put a lot of pressure on Guerrero Jr. before the 2021 season to produce and live up to expectations. He did just that, sending an early notice to everybody that he was a much different player than from the first two seasons. He got a hit in 13 of his first 14 games that season, and he was hitting the ball harder than ever before. He homered twice in the first week of the season, and by April 15th, was already hitting over .400.[ii]

On April 27th, Guerrero Jr. had his most outstanding game yet. Facing the Washington Nationals and their ace Max Scherzer with his father in attendance in Dunedin, Guerrero Jr. slammed three home runs, one of those being a grand slam. He totaled seven RBIs, breaking personal records all around.

"I'm feeling very blessed right now," Guerrero said. "Hitting two homers against a legend like that, it's unbelievable what I'm feeling right now."[xxxi]

Scherzer became only the second pitcher to allow a home run to both Guerreros during their careers. Guerrero Sr. looked on, so proud of his son, knowing how hard he had worked in the offseason and seeing his incredible transformation.

"What a day for my boy," the senior Guerrero said on his Twitter account. "All the hard work is paying off."[xxxi]

"Looking at Vladdy, he has a good eye," Nationals manager Dave Martinez said. "He doesn't chase much as Senior. That's one big difference I've noticed already, he swings at strikes."[xxxi]

Guerrero Jr. finished April hitting .350 with 7 home runs and 20 RBIs. His .663 slugging percentage led all of baseball. The power surge continued in May, where Guerrero had five 3-hit games and a string of three games in a row with a home run. He homered twice on May 21st, and then homered twice again on May 24th, both times against the Rays' tough pitching staff.

Guerrero Jr. hit 9 home runs in May, totaling 16 heading into June. And the home runs just kept coming. He homered four games in a row, all against the Red Sox, in a series from June 11th to 14th. In that four-game series, he compiled nine hits, four home runs, and eight RBIs. He bolstered his average over .350 and was among the league leaders in batting average.[ii]

Guerrero Jr. had another stretch of three straight home runs in June and hit 10 total during the month. He went into July hitting .339 with a league-best .675 slugging percentage and 26 home runs. He was an obvious selection for the American League in the All-Star Game at Coors Field in Colorado.

Guerrero Jr. started and batted third in his first-ever Mid-Summer Classic, and he did not disappoint. Facing Corbin Burnes in the top of the third, Guerrero

Jr. swung for the fences and the ball went well beyond that. He hit a mammoth home run that went 468 feet over the left center-field wall. The blast gave the American League a 2-0 lead; they would go on to win 5-2.

After the game, MLB announced Vladimir Guerrero Jr. as the All-Star Game MVP. At 22 years old, he became the youngest MVP in history. He also became the first Blue Jays player to ever win All-Star Game MVP.

"Dreams come true," Guerrero Jr. said through a translator. "Since I was a kid, I was thinking about this moment. I've worked all my life very hard and a lot of it is happening right now."[xxxii]

"I honestly just want to thank my dad," Guerrero Jr. added. "This is for you."[xxxii]

The 468-foot blast was the longest recorded All-Star Game home run according to Statcast, and it wasn't even close! Guerrero Jr. topped Kris Bryant's 410-foot shot, which was the previous longest.

"What a shot; holy moly, that was a bomb," Padres third baseman Manny Machado said. "The kid is special, man; what he's doing this year has been unbelievable to watch. To see it firsthand today, he put on a show."[xxxii]

Guerrero Jr. went into the second half of the year in MVP contention, although with the Angels' Shohei Ohtani hitting and pitching the lights out, it would be a tough honor to win that year. Guerrero Jr. slowed down some in July and August, hitting 13 home runs combined between the two months. His average also fell some, from .341 on July 7th to .311 on August 12th, diminishing his chances of winning the Triple Crown. One bright spot was that, with the COVID travel restrictions finally easing up, the Blue Jays were allowed to return to their home in Toronto to play.

On August 30th, Guerrero Jr. blasted two home runs and four RBIs in helping the Blue Jays to a 7-3 win. Those two homers meant he was going into September with 39 home runs, leading all of baseball. At 70-62, the Blue Jays were in the Wild Card hunt, although trailing their rivals.[ii]

Making the postseason would be challenging, though, given the strength of the AL East. The Tampa Bay Rays, New York Yankees, and Boston Red Sox were all having extraordinary seasons, with the three teams 20 games above .500. With the Rays beginning to pull away in the division, only two teams could make the Wild Card between Toronto, Boston, and New York.

The Blue Jays then won 12 out of 13 games to open the month to move themselves on the inside of the playoff picture, passing the Red Sox. A lot of that had to do with Guerrero Jr., who went on a 14-game hitting streak, the longest of his career. Then, in a four-game series with the Yankees, he homered three times as the Blue Jays swept the Yankees.[ii]

The Blue Jays ended the season with three straight wins, dominating Baltimore and outscoring them 22-5 in the final two games. In those last two games that they had needed to win, Guerrero Jr. got three hits, a double, and two home runs to give the Blue Jays a chance at making the playoffs. Unfortunately, 91-71 was not quite enough, as both the Yankees and Red Sox finished 92-70, besting the Blue Jays by a game to earn the Wild Card. The Rays won 100 games to easily win the division.

"It hurts," Guerrero said through a translator. "Knowing that you won 91 games and you didn't make the playoffs, it really hurts me, it hurts all my teammates. That's just going to make me stronger to come back next year even better than this year."[xxxiii]

In the final game of the year, he hit home run number 48, making him the youngest player in MLB history to hit that many homers in a season.

For Guerrero Jr., though, it was a career season. *Plákata* hit .311, driving in 111 runs and securing 29 doubles. He led the American League in seven offensive categories: home runs (48), runs scored (123), on-base percentage (.401), slugging percentage (.601), OPS (1.002), OPS+ (167), and total bases (163). In most seasons, that would be good enough to win MVP. However, Shohei Ohtani beat out Guerrero Jr., primarily because he was not just good offensively but was also an effective pitcher.

Guerrero Jr. was named to the 2021 All-MLB Team and also earned his first Silver Slugger Award. Additionally, he won the Hank Aaron Award and Tip O'Neill Award to go along with his All-Star Game MVP. Winning the Silver Slugger made Guerrero Jr.

the first Blue Jays first baseman to win the award since 2003.

"I just try to hit the ball through the middle," Guerrero Jr. said. "I don't try to hit ground balls or fly balls. I just try to hit line drives, hit it hard."[xxxiv]

Continued Success (2022-23)

On March 22, 2022, the Blue Jays and Vladimir Guerrero Jr. agreed to a $7.9-million contract, allowing the young slugger to avoid arbitration. It also prevented any distraction, as Guerrero Jr. wanted to continue the success he had built up in 2022.[xxxv]

Vlad reported to camp again in great shape and alerted the coaches that he would be open to playing third base again if called upon. The biggest issue for his poor fielding play in the past had been his fitness, and he had adapted well to his new role at first base. But he also liked the option of returning to third.

Guerrero Jr. predicted a huge year; during Spring Training, he issued a now-famous quote that said, "What we did last year was a trailer. Now you guys are going to see the movie." Of course, that put a lot of pressure on the Blue Jays to improve upon a year ago.[xxxvi]

"Our goal is to get to the World Series and win the World Series," Guerrero said through club interpreter Hector Lebron. "There's 29 other teams trying to do the same thing. That's our goal for the year, though. We're going to stay focused, work hard for everybody on the team. If we get there, we get there, and hopefully we'll win it."[xxxvi]

Trying to replicate what he did a year ago would not be easy, especially considering the way he got off to a great start in 2022. On April 13th, Guerrero Jr. and the Blue Jays traveled to the Bronx to play the Yankees and the young slugger went crazy. He went four-for-four and hit three home runs, all while playing with a deep gash on his hand. It was his second three-home run game already of his young career.

"Add that one to my list," Guerrero Jr. said when asked where this ranks among his most impressive feats.[xxxvii]

"That guy, he's a game-changer," Yankees slugger Aaron Judge said about Guerrero.

Guerrero Jr. opened April hitting .286 with 6 home runs and 16 RBIs. In May, he went on a 15-game hitting streak, the longest of his career, before enduring a 0-for-14 slump. He hit just .217 in May and totaled just three home runs.

Guerrero Jr. went into the All-Star break hitting .271 and the Blue Jays were in the thick of the Wild Card chase at 50-43. For the second straight season, Guerrero Jr. was selected to play in the All-Star Game. However, unlike a season ago, he could not replicate the same success that saw him win the MVP. He went

0-for-2 when the American League beat the National League, 3-2.[ii]

The Blue Jays bounced back from the break and went on an eight-game hitting streak, including a four-for-five performance from Guerrero Jr. against the Red Sox. Guerrero Jr. hit an impressive .340 in July with 17 RBIs and 17 runs scored and started August on a 16-game hitting streak.

The last two months for Guerrero Jr. were up and down. He did not display the same power that he did a season ago, but still came through in key moments to help the Blue Jays into the postseason for the second time in his young career. Guerrero Jr. finished the season hitting .274 with a .480 slugging percentage. After 48 home runs in 2021, he hit 32 in 2022, along with 97 RBIs and 90 runs scored. He would finish 16th in the final voting for MVP.

Defensively, though, Guerrero Jr. continued to see huge improvements. A year after making just 8 errors at first base, he made only 10 in 2022 in 128 games played at the position. He also made several stellar plays in the field throughout the year. As a result, Guerrero Jr. won the first Gold Glove of his career.

In a best-of-three series against the Mariners, Guerrero Jr. struggled, going one-for-eight in two games. The Blue Jays lost both games and were eliminated from the playoffs.

Guerrero Jr. got off to a fast start, though, in 2023. In the season's opener, he got two hits and three RBIs in Toronto's win over the Cardinals. From April 5th to April 9th, he got 13 hits in five games, including 2 home runs and 8 runs scored, propelling his average to .444 early in the season. He hit .303 in April, including five home runs.[ii]

On May 23rd against the Rays, Guerrero Jr. got three hits and six RBIs, including a home run, as the Blue Jays offense continued to shine, winning the game 20-

6. Despite a solid start, though, at 26-23, the Blue Jays were well behind the Rays in the AL East.

Guerrero Jr. kept his average near .300 for most of the first half of the season. At the end of June, he was selected to his third consecutive All-Star Game. He was also invited to appear in the Home Run Derby in Seattle, and he agreed, making it his first appearance in the Derby since his historic performance in 2019. He was seeking to join his father as the first father-son duo to win the Home Run Derby; Guerrero Sr. had won it in 2007.

"I don't remember much," Guerrero Jr. admitted Monday night thinking back to his father's performance. "I guess I was too young."[xxxviii]

Guerrero Jr. did not put up the same kind of record numbers that he did in 2019, but it was still quite a show. In the first round, he defeated Mookie Betts by hitting 26 home runs. He then faced a challenge in the semifinals, going up against hometown star Julio

Rodriguez. After Rodriguez hit 20, Guerrero Jr. topped him with 21 homers, setting up a final match with the Rays' Randy Arozarena.

Arozarena was coming off 35 home runs in the semifinals, reminiscent of Guerrero Jr.'s 40 back in 2019. Guerrero Jr. knew the feeling of hitting a lot of home runs prior to the finals, and figured Arozarena would probably be tired—and he was. Guerrero Jr. finished strong and was able to hold off a late surge by Arozarena, beating him 25 home runs to 23 in the finals.

Guerrero Jr. held up the same trophy after the Derby that his father had hoisted 16 years ago. Guerrero Jr. said afterward that he was not sure if he would compete in 2024, but if he does, he would have a chance to become only the fourth player in MLB history to win back-to-back Derbies.

Then came the Midseason Classic. Guerrero Jr. failed to get a hit for the American League as they lost to the

National League 3-2. His main focus in the second half was simply trying to make the postseason, as the Blue Jays were positioned well for a playoff push.

Guerrero Jr. hit three home runs during the second half of July, but his average remained close to .270 as he headed into August. His power numbers weren't nearly what they were a season ago. On August 24th, he had just 18 home runs as he approached the final month of the season.

Needing a strong finish, the Blue Jays went into the final two weeks in a tight battle for the playoffs with the Rangers and Mariners. With only two Wild Card spots available after the Rays had already clinched the first spot, they would have to fight their way into the postseason.

Guerrero Jr. produced, hitting home runs in three straight games against the Rangers and Red Sox in mid-September. Then, on September 24th, he hit two crucial home runs to lift the Blue Jays to a 9-5 win over the Rays. On September 29th against the Rays, he produced three hits, including two doubles, in another big win that clinched a Wild Card berth for the Blue Jays. They would take on the Twins in a best-of-three series.

But it was the same old story for the Blue Jays in the postseason, unfortunately. Their offense, which had been so strong all season long, struggled to get any traction in the playoffs. They fell behind early in Game 1 and could not rally, losing 3-1 despite a double from Guerrero Jr. Then, in Game 2, the entire offense was shut out and they lost 2-0 to end their season. Guerrero Jr. went one-for-seven in the playoffs.[ii]

Guerrero Jr. finished 2023 hitting a disappointing .264 with 26 home runs. He produced 96 RBIs and scored 78 runs while posting a .444 slugging percentage. In the field, though, Guerrero Jr. succumbed to just eight errors and produced a .991 fielding percentage.

The question heading into 2024 is, can Vladimir Guerrero Jr. return to his 2021 form? Can he get back to hitting more than 40 home runs and lead the American League offensively again? He has incredible potential to do just that, but you'll have to tune in to find out.

Chapter 5: Personal Life

Vladimir Guerrero Jr. has kept his personal life extremely private, but he recently married Nathalie Guerrero in the spring of 2023 in a secret ceremony. The two had been dating for a long time, and given that she is from Canada, the two share a lot in common. The couple has two beautiful girls, Vlymil and Vlyshil..[xxxix]

Besides taking care of her children at home, Nathalie Guerrero also manages the Vladimir Guerrero Jr. Foundation, also known as The VG27 Foundation, which was developed in 2022. The Foundation helps struggling families and their children, giving them a better life. The main focus of the charity is providing gifts and money for those in need in Vlad's home country, particularly at Christmastime. It also offers healthcare services for those who need it throughout the year.[xl]

Guerrero Jr.'s heart has always been in the right place, as he watched his father do similar work when he was a player. Guerrero Jr., inspired by him, was uplifted, and always wanted to have a foundational charity of his own one day so he could be like his dad. His dream came true in 2022.

"Our mission is to provide support to low-income children, youth, and their families, so that with our contributions we can impact their lives and impact the creation of a better future," Guerrero Jr. said.

"It's very emotional for me. I feel very grateful to do this, and I learned that from my dad," Guerrero said through an interpreter. "Since I've been a kid, he would do that all the time to help kids, help other people, help the community. I want to follow in his footsteps. There is nothing more satisfying than, every 24th of December, to give something to kids who don't have anything. When we give something to a kid, it's a feeling that I cannot describe."[xli]

During Christmas 2022, Guerrero Jr. and his family distributed meals to over 1,000 families in need during the holiday season back home in the Dominican Republic.

"When I was younger, it was a blessing," Guerrero said. "Because of my dad, we celebrated Christmas with everything, a lot of food, lots of toys. I think that's the reason I am like that with kids in my community. When I give a gift to one kid, it feels like my dad giving a gift to me. It's a blessing."[xlii]

The Guerrero Jr. family also distributes during Three Kings Day, a popular holiday in the Dominican Republic celebrated on January 6th. The tradition, similar to Christmas, is when children receive gifts from adults.

Guerrero Jr.'s contributions to his Foundation and other charities led him to be recently nominated for the Roberto Clemente Award. He also regularly contributes to the Jays Care Foundation, which promotes gender equality and fair opportunities for girls seeking to play sports. It also seeks to provide money to girls recreational programs so they have better facilities, just like the boys do, and helps families that are underprivileged and need assistance.

In December 2023, Guerrero Jr. traveled to Puerto Rico, teaming up with Jose Berrios for a Charity Softball Game and Home Run Derby. Team Guerrero won 14-9 in the charity game, but the big highlight was the Home Run Derby. Playing with a metal bat, the balls were flying out of the park faster and deeper than ever. Guerrero Jr. won the Derby on the final swing of the night, beating the Guardians' Jonathan Rodriguez.

The money raised during the event went to the Berrios' La MaKina Foundation, a charity that helps raise money for young people facing a difficult life.

"This is very special for me," Guerrero Jr. said. "When you talk about teammates, you're talking about family.

When [Berríos] asked me in June, I told him of course I would do it. When it comes to someone like José Berrios, I'm always going to say yes."[xlii]

One of the most notable features about Guerrero Jr. is his private and humble demeanor. He is not one to boast on social media about his philanthropy or really anything that's going on around him; it's one reason why not a lot of people even know about his family life with Nathalie and his kids. He keeps things very close to him, and when he plays baseball, he lets his bat do the talking and lets his smile take care of the rest.

"Vladdy is really someone that doesn't want to expose his private life that much," Hall-of-Fame pitcher Pedro Martinez said, who is also from the Dominican Republic. "He isn't interested in cameras. He is just a human being that did what he had to do without expecting to be seen by anybody else. You drop him in the field, he knows what to do right away. He's wide awake and he will tell you, 'Get me a bat and I know what to do with that ball; get me a glove and I know how to catch.' But for him to go out there and explain it—I don't think so. No. Vladdy did it his own way, a very unique way, and he is the same way in his life. Nobody would know unless you get to know him really well and you spend a lot of time with him."[v]

In other words, Guerrero Jr. is as real as you get, and sometimes, those are the best guys to idolize. He doesn't do things for the camera but instead for himself, his family, and the fans. He is his own person and wants to be known that way.

"When you see that name Guerrero on the back of the jersey, you can make assumptions about who he is," Cesar Martin said, a Dominican native and Guerrero Jr.'s former manager with the Lansing Lugnuts. "But he never asked to be treated differently. He doesn't just want to talk to the Spanish-speaking players. He goes out of his way to include everyone. He doesn't think he's special. He works like he's trying to prove something. He plays like he's poor."[xiv]

Nothing Beats Family

Vladimir Guerrero Jr.'s life growing up was nothing like his father's. While his father was forced to live off scraps and work his way to success, Guerrero Jr. had it all laid out for him. But that doesn't mean he forgets about what his family had to go through for him to get where he was.

"I can only imagine what my family's life was like when they needed help," Guerrero Jr. said through a translator. "It wasn't easy for them. They made sacrifices. I benefited from that. I got to live my life because of all that came before me."[xiv]

Guerrero Jr. spends much of his offseason time where he grew up in the Dominican. He loves spending time with his father and talking about the old days. He helps out his Uncle Wilton at his baseball camp, working with young athletes who aspire to be just like him. The rest of the time is spent with his own family.

The weekends in the winter were mostly reserved for softball, although when Guerrero Jr. went to Toronto and started a family of his own, it wasn't played as much. Since they were younger, they would always set up a field together and try and outdo the other with friends and family. Guerrero Sr. says he has a hard time keeping up with his son's speed.

"But that's because he's younger," Guerrero Sr. said. "Hitting, though? I try to show him I still have it."[xiv]

Family no doubt plays a big role in Guerrero Jr.'s life. In addition to Vladdy's wife and kids, his father, and his uncle, his grandmother has been there every step of the way as well, particularly in the kitchen. Some call her the most powerful grandmother in baseball, making food not just for her grandson but the entire Blue Jays team. Sometimes, other players from other teams ask Guerrero Jr. if she can cook for them; she doesn't turn anyone down if her grandson asks.

"I do it out of love," Grandma Altagracia said.[xliii]

It's been a tradition for Altagracia. She cooked for all four of her sons, who all made it to the professional leagues, and Vladimir Sr. and Wilton played in the majors. She's carried the tradition on for her grandson, Vladimir Jr., and clearly dotes on him. Because he has so much love and respect for his grandparents and wants to be around them more, Vladimir Jr. even invited them to move in with him to his Toronto home during the season. They couldn't turn down the opportunity to be "Chef Abuela."

"As long as I have strength in me, I have to give that strength to them," Altagracia said of her grandchildren. "So, I've dedicated myself to this."[xiv]

Altagracia must certainly be a wonderful cook— after all, it was all her delicious cooking that got Vladdy into a bit of trouble with his weight gain during

COVID! But she doesn't just help her grandson in the kitchen, showing him how to cook the most delicious meals; she also helps him personally. Whenever he has a bad game and comes home upset, she calms him down and puts the smile back on his face. If he complains about a bad call, she says he has to accept it and respect it.

"She always tells me to respect the game and to respect my teammates," Guerrero Jr. said.[xiv]

Since 2020, Guerrero Jr. has spruced up his workout regimen, focusing on exercise more than ever before. As we all know, those extra pounds can be awfully easy to put on and excruciatingly hard to get off, especially when you are a foodie! Guerrero Jr. is clearly that, but he realized after 2019 that he couldn't just show up heavy and succeed; he had to make fitness a big part of his life.

"I like to compete, so I took the workouts as a challenge," he said. "Now, on the other hand, the sacrifices that I had to make were obviously the food. I had to cut down going to my favorite places. In the Dominican, I like to go to the beach to relax, eat there. I had cut all that stuff to make sure that I was going to be ready for business."[xliv]

That meant he couldn't eat foods that he traditionally loves. As for the hardest food he had to cut out? It was undoubtedly anything with rice.

"There are some dishes that you have to eat with rice, but I cut that," Guerrero said. "Instead of rice, I'd eat salad, and seeing everyone else eating rice is kind of hard, you know? But those are things I had to do to get better and I did."[xlv]

"Sometimes you don't realize you need to make a change until it kind of hits you in the face," coach John Schneider said. "We didn't try to force that on him in the minors, but we tried to make him very aware of how important all that stuff was. And it was a combination of him figuring that out and then him tackling it head-on."[xlv]

By spending a lot of time shedding weight in the offseason and making fitness a big part of his personal life, Guerrero Jr. did what many people thought was impossible in 2019—he won a Gold Glove, and at a different position than what he was signed for. That helped to boost his popularity and growing interest in him, not just by fans and the media but also by those looking to market him.

Guerrero Jr. has been an endorsement machine. Since 2019, he has signed deals with companies like Wilson, Topps, Chevrolet Canada, Smuckers, Xbox Canada, BIGS Sunflower Seeds, and Jordan. He is also featured in the promotions for the latest *MLB The Show* video game.

Guerrero Jr. will make $19.9 million with the Blue Jays in 2024 and is signed on through 2026. His current net worth is $5 million.[xlv]

Chapter 6: Legacy

Vladimir Guerrero Jr. has worked hard to build his own legacy and life separate from his father's. He wants to make his own name and be known as Vladimir Guerrero Jr., not "Vladimir Guerrero's son." However, that does not mean he isn't grateful for his father. He does everything for him, wanting to make him proud. The two spend a lot of time together in the offseason, with Vladimir Sr. giving his son small pieces of advice to help him succeed.

"¿Mi papá? He's my everything," Guerrero Jr. said. "I want to show people what I can do, that I'm not here because of my name."[xiv]

"I never talk to him about expectations," Guerrero Sr. said about his son. "I've told him, 'Don't listen to what people say; play your game.'"[xiv]

Comparing the two careers of father and son is premature thus far, as Vladdy is still young and undoubtedly has a long career ahead of him. However, there are still some parallels that we can point out. Both men finished sixth in their first season for Rookie of the Year. Guerrero Jr. hit 15 home runs and 69 RBIs in 123 games, while his father hit 12 home runs and just 41 RBIs in 99 games. Many of their numbers are nearly identical, including slugging percentage and on-base percentage.[ii]

Guerrero Sr., though, had a better batting average through his first five years and showcased more power. Guerrero Sr. hit over .300 every single season from 1997 to 2008, while Guerrero Jr. has hit over .300 just once in his first five years. In his first four seasons, Guerrero Sr. hit 136 home runs, while Guerrero Jr. has hit 130 homers in five full seasons (note: 2020 was a shortened year).

Guerrero Jr.'s 2021 season cannot be forgotten, however, where he led in seven offensive categories and finished No. 2 in MVP voting. His 48 home runs that year was more than any his father ever hit in a single season. Additionally, his 123 runs scored was only topped once by his father later in his career, and Guerrero Sr. did not finish in the top five for MVP voting until 2002, more than six years into his career.

Of course, Guerrero Jr. hasn't produced the same kind of numbers since 2021, but he is encouraged by his father's trajectory, who saw his best numbers several years into his career, which indicates that his own best years are likely still to come. From 2002 to 2007, seven years in, Guerrero Sr. won the MVP once and finished in the top 5 four times. Additionally, he had three seasons wherein he compiled over 200 hits, something Vladimir Jr. has yet to accomplish.[i]

So, in some ways, the son has eclipsed the father, and in other ways, Vladdy still has much to accomplish. But it's a different game today than it was then, and it is also hard to compare the two because Vladimir Jr. also started playing at 19 years old, while his father's rookie season was not until he was 22. Junior has already set records in the Home Run Derby and his 48 home runs in one season is the most for any player 22 years old or younger.

In 2021, Senior and Junior made history when Vladimir Jr. finished runner-up for MVP. While it would have been nice to win the award like his father did, they became the first father-son duo to finish in the top 2 in any significant BBWAA Award (MVP, Rookie of the Year, Cy Young). They already hold the distinction as the first father and son duo to win the Home Run Derby.[xlvi]

But it's not just about father and son; the family legacy is quite strong as well. Guerrero Sr. is already in the Hall of Fame, while his son is already beginning to put together a noteworthy resume that could eventually see him get there as well. Meanwhile, Vladimir Sr.'s brother, Wilton, played eight years in the major leagues, mostly with the Nationals and Dodgers. The third brother of the group, Julio, was part of the Red

Sox organization for four years. Gabriel Guerrero, the cousin of Vladimir Sr., spent most of his time in the minors with the Mariners and Reds and was brought up to the big leagues briefly in 2018.[xlvii]

Vladimir Jr.'s brother Pablo is already making a name for himself, signed by the Texas Rangers at just 16 years old. He is currently an international player in the Dominican League and should debut in the U.S. fairly soon as a minor league rookie. Their half-brother, Vladi Miguel, was also recently signed by the New York Mets organization and is just 17 years old. And then there is also Vladdy's youngest half-brother Pedro, who, at just 12 years old, is already tearing up the field and garnering some comparisons to his dad, Vlad Sr. Furthermore, even Vladimir Jr.'s cousin Gregory played in the Mets organization from 2016 to 2022. Undoubtedly, that's some very special DNA coursing through the Guerrero family!

But trying to top the legacies of the two Vladimirs will be difficult, especially as Junior continues to put together stellar seasons. In 2021, Guerrero Jr. became the first Blue Jays player in history to lead the league in both on-base percentage and slugging. He also became the youngest player to win the home run title.

Guerrero Jr.'s biggest goal is to bring a World Series to Toronto. He's mentioned it repeatedly over the years, including saying the 2021 season was just a movie trailer to the big show. However, Guerrero Jr. and the Blue Jays have since failed to get past the Wild Card round. The biggest obstacle in their way is perhaps their formidable division counterparts; Baltimore and Tampa Bay have the kind of farm systems that will keep them among the best in the American League for a long time, and the Yankees and Red Sox have proven in the past that they are willing to pay big money to propel them into contention. The Blue Jays do not have those deep pockets, but they do have *Plákata*!

Undoubtedly, Guerrero Jr. is a fierce competitor, and he knows what other Latin American players around him are doing as well. In fact, he strives to keep up with them. He regularly talks to and monitors the accomplishments of peers like Ronald Acuna Jr., Fernando Tatis Jr., and Juan Soto, all of whom are players he has tremendous respect for. Acuna Jr.'s success has undoubtedly motivated Guerrero Jr.

Of course, it is too early to tell if Guerrero Jr. will ultimately join his father in the Hall of Fame. Five years in the league isn't much of a barometer, and Junior is only 24 years old. He still has at least 10 more years in his prime to go. From a home run perspective, *Plákata* is certainly on the right track. Trying to get to 500 homers will be a career goal of his. Since his 48-home run season, he's dropped in production to 32 and 26, respectively, in 2022 and 2023. In 2024, it will be crucial to get those home run numbers up again.

He will want to try and pull his average up as well; currently, he is hitting just .279 in his career, with four of his five seasons including averages of .274 or less. (Of course, part of that is due to his early subpar seasons in 2019 and 2020. He also has just one season with over 100 RBIs. In comparison, his father had 10 seasons of more than 100 RBIs in a season.

So, there's obviously work to do. But Vladamir Guerrero Jr. undoubtedly has a promising future, and his career will be one that will be very exciting to watch unfold in the years to come.

Conclusion

There is perhaps no greater pressure put on an athlete than when you are the son of a father who is in the Hall of Fame. Vladimir Guerrero Jr. was pegged to be a major leaguer from the day he posed with his father in a Montreal Expos jersey at three years old. But the way he has handled those lofty expectations, the maturation he's shown, and the positive attitude he always displays on the field has helped him create his own story and identity.

"I'm so happy and I'm so proud of him that he didn't let his career go somewhere else instead of grabbing it," Blue Jays third base coach Luis Rivera said. "He knows the expectations that were put on him. He's very, very mature about handling everything that is thrown at him. He continued to be the same guy. He wasn't afraid; he wasn't complaining about all the expectations that people were putting on him. You know what he did? He went, 'Okay, this is what people expect from me? I expect that from me, also.'"xlv

Vladimir Guerrero Jr. taught us the importance of creating your own story, but to make it, you have to put in incredibly hard work. In fact, Guerrero Jr. could have had an easy life, probably having to work very little and just live off the money from his father. But what makes his story so much better is that he did have money but was still motivated to try and be the best baseball player ever from his home country, and to wear a Toronto Blue Jays uniform. He epitomizes what it means to love the game of baseball in its purest sense.

"Obviously people look from the outside and see someone who's very gifted and that obviously is blessed with a lot of ability," Bo Bichette said about his teammate. "But the work that he puts in, his desire to be the best player on the field every day, I think that not only pushes me, but pushes the rest of the team.

He's also taught me how to have fun on the field. I've always been very serious about the game, and I still am. He's definitely taught me, it's OK to smile, it's OK to jump around, hug your teammates, show love to everybody."[vii]

Vladimir Guerrero Jr.'s love for his teammates is obvious, and he wants to take his team to the pinnacle of success by being the greatest baseball player he can be. While the jury's still out on whether he can make that happen, he is moving in the right direction. And not only that, but he is having fun doing it and making those around him better and happier ballplayers in the process. He is exactly the kind of person you always want on your team and by your side.

Final Word/About the Author

Wow! You made it to the end of this book, and you're reading the About the Author section? Now that's impressive and puts you in the top 1% of readers.

Since you're curious about me, I was born and raised in Norwalk, Connecticut. Growing up, I could often be found spending many nights watching basketball, soccer, and football matches with my father in the family living room. I love sports and everything that sports can embody. I believe that sports are one of the most genuine forms of competition, heart, and determination. I write my works to learn more about influential athletes in the hopes that from my writing, you the reader can walk away inspired to put in an equal if not greater amount of hard work and perseverance to pursue your goals.

I've written these stories for over a decade, and loved every moment of it. When I look back on my life, I am most proud of not just having covered so many different athletes' inspirational stories, but for all the times I got e-mails or handwritten letters from readers on the impact my books have had on them.

So thank you from the bottom of my heart for allowing me to do work I find meaningful. I am incredibly grateful for you and your support.

If you're new to my sports biography books, welcome. I have goodies for you as a thank you from me in the pages ahead.

Before we get there though, I have a question for you…

Were you inspired at any point in this book?
If so, would you help someone else get inspired too?

You see, my mission is to inspire sports fans of all ages around the world that anything is possible through hard work and perseverance…but the only way to accomplish this mission is by reaching everyone.

So here's my ask from you:

Most people, regardless of what the saying tells them to do, judge a book by its cover (and its reviews).

If you enjoyed *Vladimir Guerrero Jr.: The Inspiring Story of One of Baseball's Star First Basemen,* please help inspire another person needing to hear this story by leaving a review.

Doing so takes less than a minute, and that dose of inspiration can change another person's life in more ways than you can even imagine.

To get that generous 'feel good' feeling and help another person, all you have to do is take 60 seconds and leave a review.

If you're on Audible: hit the three dots in the top right of your device, click rate & review, then leave a few sentences about the book with a star rating.

If you're reading on Kindle or an e-reader: scroll to the bottom of the book, then swipe up and it will prompt a review for you.

If for some reason these have changed: you can head back to Amazon and leave a review right on the book's page.

Thank you for helping another person, and for your support of my writing as an independent author.

Clayton

Like what you read?
Then you'll love these too!

This book is one of hundreds of stories I've written. If you enjoyed this story on Vladimir Guerrero Jr., you'll love my other sports biography book series too.

You can find them by visiting my website at claytongeoffreys.com or by scanning the QR code below to follow my author page on Amazon.

SCAN ME

Here's a little teaser about each of my sports biography book series:

Baseball Biography Books: This series covers the stories of over 40 MLB greats such as Aaron Judge, Shohei Ohtani, Mike Trout, and more.

Basketball Biography Books: This series covers the stories of over 100 NBA greats such as Stephen Curry, LeBron James, Michael Jordan, and more.

Football Biography Books: This series covers the stories of over 50 NFL greats such as Peyton Manning, Tom Brady, and Patrick Mahomes, and more.

Basketball Leadership Biography Books: This series covers the stories of basketball coaching greats such as Steve Kerr, Gregg Popovich, John Wooden, and more.

Soccer Biography Books: This series covers the stories of tennis greats such as Neymar, Harry Kane, Robert Lewandowski, and more.

Tennis Biography Books: This series covers the stories of tennis greats such as Serena Williams, Rafael Nadal, Andy Roddick, and more.

Women's Basketball Biography Books: This series covers the stories of many WNBA greats such as Diana Taurasi, Sue Bird, Sabrina Ionescu, and more.

Lastly, if you'd like to join my exclusive list where I let you know about my latest books, and gift you free copies of some of my other books, go to **claytongeoffreys.com/goodies**.

Or, if you don't like typing, scan the following QR code here to go there directly. See you there!

Clayton

References

[i] "Vladimir Guerrero Stats." *Baseball-Reference.com.* Nd. Web.

[ii] "Vladimir Guerrero Jr. Stats." *Baseball-Reference.com.* Nd. Web.

[iii] Gordon, Devin. "Inside the Breathtaking Rise of Vladimir Guerrero Jr." *ESPN.com.* 15 Sep 2021. Web.

[iv] Singh, David. "Money. Fame. Power. Hitter." *SportsNet Canada.* 2023. Web.

[v] Brunt, Stephen. "In the Kingdom of the Guerreros." *SportsNet Canada.* 2023. Web.

[vi] Sandler, Tracy. "5 Fun Facts About Vladimir Guerrero Jr." *FGSN.com.* 29 Sep 2021. Web.

[vii] Robson, Dan and McGrath, Kaitlyn. "Born To Play Baseball: Blue Jays Vladimir Guerrero Jr. Making a Name for Himself Amid Playoff Chase." *The Athletic.* 29 Sep 2021. Web.

[viii] Armstrong, Laura. "Vlad to the Bone." *The Star.* 25 Apr 2019. Web.

[ix] MacLeod, Robert. "Vladimir Guerrero Gears up for Major League Debut." *TheGlobeandMail.com.* 25 Apr 2019. Web.

[x] Lott, John. "Toronto Blue Jays Make it Official, Sign Vladimir Guerrero Jr." *NationalPost.com.* 2 Jul 2015. Web.

[xi] Blair, Jeff. "Son of a Gun." *SportsNet.ca.* 5 Jun 2016. Web.

[xii] Lott, John. "The Legend of Vladimir Guerrero Jr. Keeps Growing." *Vice.com.* 6 Apr 2016. Web.

[xiii] Rosenbaum, Mike. "Like Father, Like Home Run: Dad Sees Vlad Jr. Jack." *MLB.com.* 24 Jun 2016. Web.

[xiv] Sanchez, Robert. "Vlad Guerrero Jr. Is Trying to Live Up to His Famous Name." *ESPN.com.* 10 Aug 2017. Web.

[xv] Lott, John. "The Vladimir Guerrero Jr. Show Has Begun." *Vice.com.* 27 Jun 2016. Web.

[xvi] Passan, Jeff. "Prospect Heat Check: Is MLB Prodigy Ready for a 19-Year-Old Hitting Prodigy?" *Yahoo Sports.* 1 May 2018. Web.

[xvii] Tayler, Jon. "Welcome to the New Era: 19-Year-Old Vladimir Guerrero Jr. Is Baseball's Most Exciting Prospect." *Sports Illustrated.* 24 May 2018. Web.

[xviii] Badler, Ben. "Simply the Best: Vladimir Guerrero Jr. is Baseball America's 2018 Minor League Player of the Year." *Baseball America.* 7 Sep 2018. Web.

[xix] Bumbaca, Chris. "Vlad Jr. For Bisons ... Again." *MiLB.com.* 10 Aug 2018. Web.

[xx] Glier, Ray. "Minor League Player of the Year: Vladimir Guerrero Jr.

Following In His Father's Footsteps." *USA Today.* 5 Sep 2018. Web.

[xxi] Cannon, Jay. "Vladimir Guerrero Jr., One of MLB's Top Prospects, Out Three Weeks With Oblique Strain." *USA Today.* 10 Mar 2019. Web.

[xxii] Couto, Melissa. "Blue Jays Call Up Top Prospect Vladimir Guerrero Jr." *CBC.ca.* 24 Apr 2019. Web.

[xxiii] "Blue Jays Introduce Vladimir Guerrero Jr. Ahead of Major League Debut." *SportsNet.ca.* 26 Apr 2019. Web.

[xxiv] "Guerrero Debuts With Hit That Sets up Jays 4-2 Win Over A's." *ESPN.com.* 26 Apr 2019. Web.

[xxv] "Drury's 3-Run HR in 11th Sparks Jays to Season Sweep of A's." *ESPN.com.* 28 Apr 2019. Web.

[xxvi] "Guerrero Jr. Hits 2 HRs, Blue Jays Beat Giants 7-3." *ESPN.com.* 15 May 2014.

[xxvii] Toribio, Juan. "Vlad Jr. Sets Records in Stunning Derby Display." *MLB.com.* 9 Jul 2019. Web.

[xxviii] "Guerrero Jr.'s Grand Slam Helps Blue Jays Beat Tigers 7-5." *ESPN.com.* 20 Jul 2019. Web.

[xxix] "Guerrero Belts Slam To Cap Blue Jays' 9-2 Rout of Royals." *ESPN.com.* 31 Jul 2019. Web.

[xxx] Ashbourne, Nick. "Vladimir Guerrero Jr.'s Rookie Season Can Only Be Described As a Disappointment." *Yahoo Sports.* 3 Oct 2019. Web.

[xxxi] "Guerrero Jr. Hits 3 HRs, Slam Off Scherzer, Jays Beat Nats." *ESPN.com.* 27 Apr 2017. Web.

[xxxii] Feinsand, Mark. "Vlad Youngest MVP After ASG HR for Ages." *MLB.com.* 14 Jul 2021. Web.

[xxxiii] "Blue Jays Rout Orioles But Get No Help, Miss Playoffs." *ESPN.com.* 3 Oct 2021. Web.

[xxxiv] Bannon, Mitch. "3 Blue Jays Win AL Silver Slugger Awards." *SI.com.* 11 Nov 2021. Web.

[xxxv] Kasabian, Paul. "Report: Vladimir Guerrero Jr., Blue Jays Agree to $7.9 Million Contract To Avoid Arbitration." *Bleacher Report.* 22 Mar 2022. Web.

[xxxvi] Matheson, Keegan. "Vlad Jr.: 'Now You Guys Are Going To See the Movie.'" *MLB.com.* 17 Mar 2022. Web.

[xxxvii] "Guerrero Slugs 3 HRs Despite Gash on Hand, Jays Beat Yankees." *ESPN.com.* 13 Apr 2022. Web.

[xxxviii] Stark, Jayson. "Vladimir Guerrero Jr. Was Born To Hit Bombs." *The Athletic.* 11 Jul 2023. Web.

[xxxix] Thapa, Utsana. "Vladimir Guerrero Jr. and Wife Nathalie Are Raising Two Kids." *PlayersBio.com.* 25 May 2023. Web.

[xl] "Vladimir Guerrero Jr. Has Laid His Foundation for the VG27." 10 Mar 2022. Web.

[xli] Matheson, Keegan. "Family Tradition Leads Guerrero Jr. To Clemente Nomination." *MLB.com.* 17 Sep 2023. Web.

[xlii] Gallegos, Martin. "Berrios, Vlad Jr. Support Youth With Charity Softball Game." *MLB.com.* 10 Dec 2023. Web.

[xliii] Wagner, James. "Abuela, Chef, Boss: Vladimir Guerrero Jr.'s Grandmother Feeds the Majors." *New York Times.* 25 Aug 2019. Web.

[xliv] Davidi, Shi. "From Promising to Promised One." *SportsNet.ca.* Nd. Web.

[xlv] "Vladimir Guerrero Jr. Net Worth." *Celebritynetworth.com.* Nd. Web.

[xlvi] Borkowski, Nathan. "Toronto Blue Jays: Revisiting Vladimir Guerrero Jr.'s Historic 2021 Season." *SportsKeeda.com.* 17 Mar 2022. Web.

[xlvii] "Be On the Lookout For Another Guerrero In the Majors." *BaseballRelatives.com.* Nd. Web.

Printed in Great Britain
by Amazon